FUN FOOD TO TICKLE YOUR MOOD

A Cookbook For Children Who Cherish The Earth

by Marko Ellinger

"YOU ARE WHAT YOU EAT" Gaylord Hauser

Cover Illustration: Mike Krone
Illustrations: Mike Krone and Judy Panek
Design and Production: Valerie Thatcher Design

© Copyright 1992 Piccadilli Press, P.O. Box 50515, Austin, Texas, (512) 453-2051 All rights reserved. No part of this book may be reproduced without written permission of the publisher.

ISBN 0-9630147-5-7

Contents

Introduction
8   Get To Know Your Kitchen
10 The Safest Tools
12 My Favorite Ingredients

Food Without Fire/Flameless Cooking
14 Yogurt Cheese
15 The Story Of Yogurt
16 Juicy Salad Dressing
17 Peeled Salad
18 Brick Sandwiches
20 The Legend Of Tea
20 Sun Burned Tea

Blast Off In The Microwave
22 Corn Cob Hob Nob
22 Grandfather Corn
23 Historic Corn
24 Spectacular Spud Bar
25 Potatoes of the Past
26 Blasted Bananas
27 The Total Banana
28 Whirlwind Chicken

At Home On The Range/Cooking On The Stove
30 Deviled Eggs
32 The Centrifugal Force
32 Marbled Eggs
33 Lava Sauce
34 Runaway Filet
36 Asparagus Tepees
38 Chili Sundaes
39 Noodle Twister
40 Fiesta Pie
42 Righteous Rigatoni

Becoming A Food Ambassador/
Recipes From Far Away Lands
44 Spring Rolls From Viet Nam
46 Spaghetti Frittata From Italy
48 Checkered Quesadillas From Mexico
50 Spice Island Muffins From Indonesia
51 The Origin Of Cloves
52 Triangles of Egypt

Edible Art/Beautiful Food You Can Eat
54 Hobgoblins
55 Green Haired Scallion
56 Carrot Turbans
57 Shrunken Heads
58 Undercover Shrimp Boat
60 Radish Mice
61 The Story of Jack o' Lantern
61 Radish Jacks
62 Pastamobile
63 Cucumber Flowers
64 Captured Green Beans
65 Designer Beans
66 Fruit Flag Pizza
68 Porcupine Pears
69 Banana Fingers
70 Sea Creatures

Dessert Chemistry
72 Pineapple Upside Down Cake
74 Coo-Coo for Coconut
76 Ginger Bread With Lemon Sauce
78 Tummy Mummy

Playing With Food
80 Carrot Sonata
81 Counterfeit Pizza
82 Organize A Kids Cook-Off
83 The Gravitational Egg
84 Eggs On Your Breath
85 Orange Neck Mutha
86 Camouflage

Cherish The Earth
88 Pesticides
89 Recycle And Save A Tree
90 Compost Garden
92 Rainmaker

Glossary

Dear Parents, Grandparents, Teachers, and Adult Cooking Cohorts,

I wrote this book to encourage children to explore the culinary arts. As an applied science, cooking is a marvelous way to develop both academic and social skills.

The recipes in this book create opportunities to apply concepts in measurement, spatial relationships, time management, vocabulary, nutrition, ecology, history, and visual art. These experiences with food will also create an awareness of environmental issues, with specific tasks kids can perform to make the world a cleaner and safer place to live.

Cooking can also help children in their emotional, social, and cultural development. The preparation of good food enhances children's self worth and self reliance, encourages a richer bond with family and friends, and creates an awareness and respect for cultural differences.

You may also find that cooking helps cure a picky eater. Children are often more interested in and appreciative of a particular dish if they get closer to its source. They are far less likely to reject food that they have grown in their gardens or made in their own kitchens.

This book puts the health and well being of your child first and foremost. All of these recipes can be mastered without the use of sharp knives. Although I recommend parental supervision at first, I believe your children will become self-sufficient, and eventually learn to cook for themselves.

Gone are the days when it was enough to make food taste and look good. Now it must also be convenient, cost effective, energy efficient, and actually good for you. We affect the earth with every bite of food that we eat. What you buy makes a tremendous difference not just for the health of your family but for the health of the planet.

I am delighted to offer you and your kids fun food I have discovered in my years as a culinary artist. I hope you enjoy using this book as an opportunity for some truly happy times with your family.

Sharing good food is an expression of love around the world! It promotes healing at every level of our consciousness. It is truly a celebration of life.

Marko Ellinger

To Every Kid Who Likes To Cook,

In this book you can learn to make music with carrots, perform magic with eggs, play games with food, and learn fun food stories. Although I may not be with you in person as you learn to cook, we will be sharing lots of fun ideas. Feel free to write if you have any questions on recipes or if you'd like to share stories of your kitchen.

- Keep in mind that these recipes can be changed. If you want to add something or take something out, do it! You are the chef! Great things have been discovered when people run out of one ingredient and use another.
- Remember to taste food as you're cooking to make sure you're on the right track. You may need to adjust a recipe if you want it to be spicier or sweeter.
- Keep the kitchen as clean as you can and put everything away after you use it so you will be given permission to cook again.
- If you see a word in this book that you don't understand, look it up in the glossary section on page 93.
- If you see a tool in a recipe that you don't understand, look it up on page 10 or 11.

Remember to have fun when you cook because the food will taste better!

Marko Ellinger

Why Kids Cook
Here are some reasons why kids say they like to cook.
1. I take my lunch to school and I want to make it myself.
2. I want to learn how to cook things I like to eat.
3. It makes me feel more independent.
4. It's a fun thing to do with my friends.
5. I learn a lot of interesting stories about food.
6. I find out about new foods I like.
7. I like all the smells and colors.

Pyramid Power

In this "Eating Right" pyramid, developed by the U.S. Department of Agriculture, the Grain and Cereal group and the Fruit and Vegetable groups occupy more space and are more important. This means that you should eat more servings from these groups than from the Meat and Dairy groups. You should limit what you eat from the Oil and Fats group.

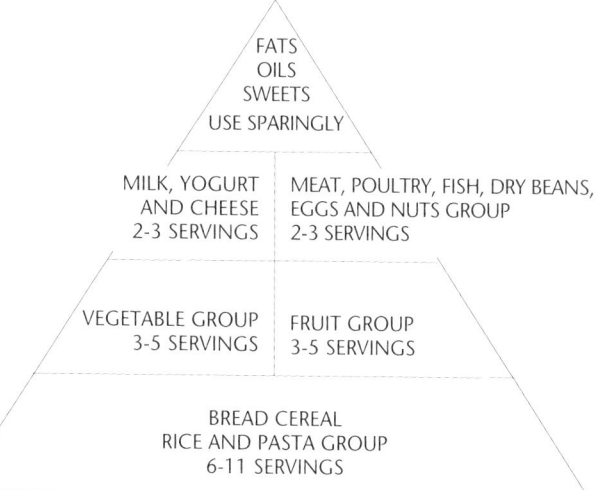

THE EATING RIGHT PYRAMID
A Guide To Daily Food Choices

FATS
OILS
SWEETS
USE SPARINGLY

MILK, YOGURT AND CHEESE
2-3 SERVINGS

MEAT, POULTRY, FISH, DRY BEANS, EGGS AND NUTS GROUP
2-3 SERVINGS

VEGETABLE GROUP
3-5 SERVINGS

FRUIT GROUP
3-5 SERVINGS

BREAD CEREAL RICE AND PASTA GROUP
6-11 SERVINGS

Feeling good doesn't just happen by accident, it's something people choose to do. Here are three good reasons to eat the right food:

1. You get sick less often.
2. It's easier to pay attention in school.
3. You have more energy.

Get to Know Your Kitchen

1. **Organizing Tools and Supplies**
   Learn where everything lives in your kitchen. Find everything you need before you cook.

2. **Clean As Can Be**
   - Always wash your hands before you work with food.
   - Clean as you cook.
   - Always clean any surface that touches meat or fish right away before you use it to prepare other food.

3. **Safe and Sound**
   - Use pot holders or oven mitts whenever you cook with heat.
   - Keep pot handles turned toward the back of the stove.
   - Use a step stool if you are not tall enough to reach the stove or counter.
   - Never use sharp knives without your parents' permission or supervision.

4. **Your Stove: Electric or Gas?**
   - Find out what kind of stove you have in your kitchen. Electric burners use coils that stay hot even after you have turned them off. Remove pots and pans from burners after you have finished cooking. Never touch these burners!
   - Gas stoves use pilot lights to ignite burners. Ask an adult to show you where the pilot lights are so you can always check to see that they're lit. If a pilot light is out, ask an adult for help!

5. Microwave Ovens

- Only use special microwave pans, not foil or metal plates.
- Don't fill cooking containers more than 3/4 full to keep food from boiling over.
- Cover your food with glass lids or plastic wrap so it won't dry out. If you use plastic wrap make sure it doesn't touch the food while it's cooking. Rotate food. Cook foods for half the time that is called for in the recipe, then turn dish 45 degrees (a quarter circle). Then finish cooking for the remaining half of the time. If you have a dish that calls for 6 minutes, cook for 3 minutes, then turn dish and cook for 3 more minutes (3+3 = 6).
- After the timer goes off, the heat continues to cook your food. Allow three minutes or longer "standing time" for your dish to finish cooking.

6. Leftovers

- Let leftovers cool down before you put them in the refrigerator.
- Wrap leftovers with plastic or foil so that they won't dry out.
- Keep the temperature inside of your refrigerator below 40 degrees. You can use a thermometer to make sure the temperature is correct.
- Never store open cans in the refrigerator.

10

Safe Tools

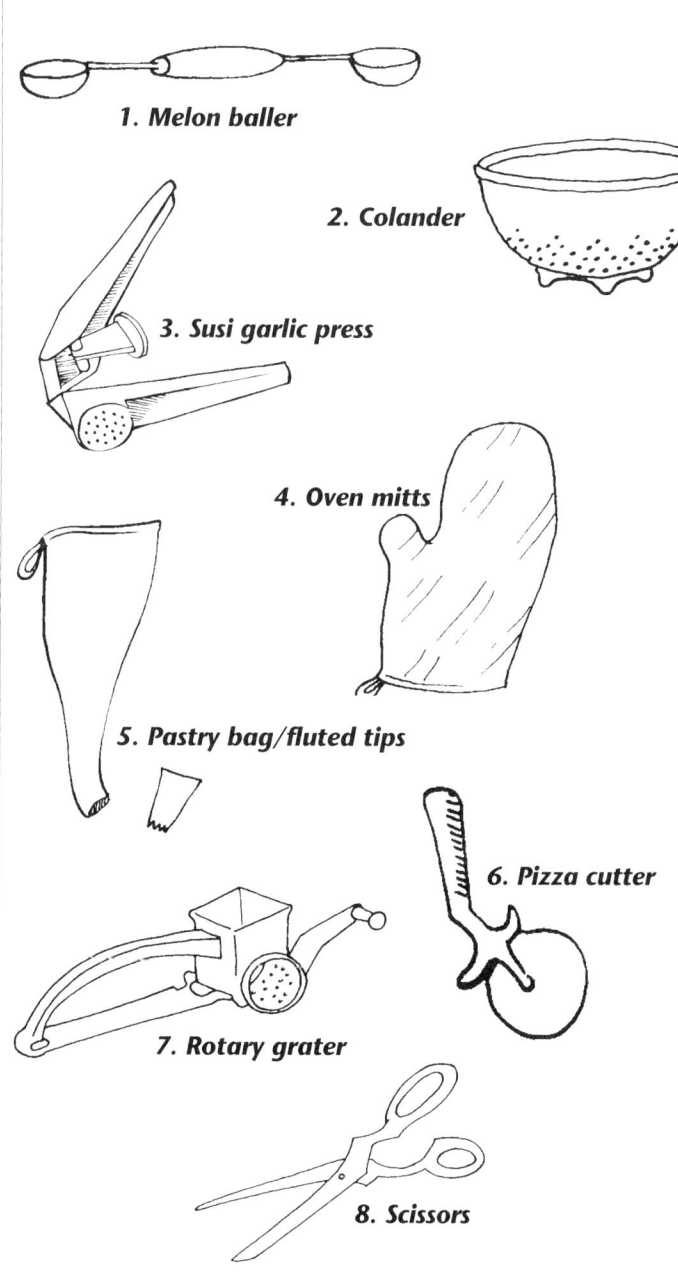

1. Melon baller
2. Colander
3. Susi garlic press
4. Oven mitts
5. Pastry bag/fluted tips
6. Pizza cutter
7. Rotary grater
8. Scissors

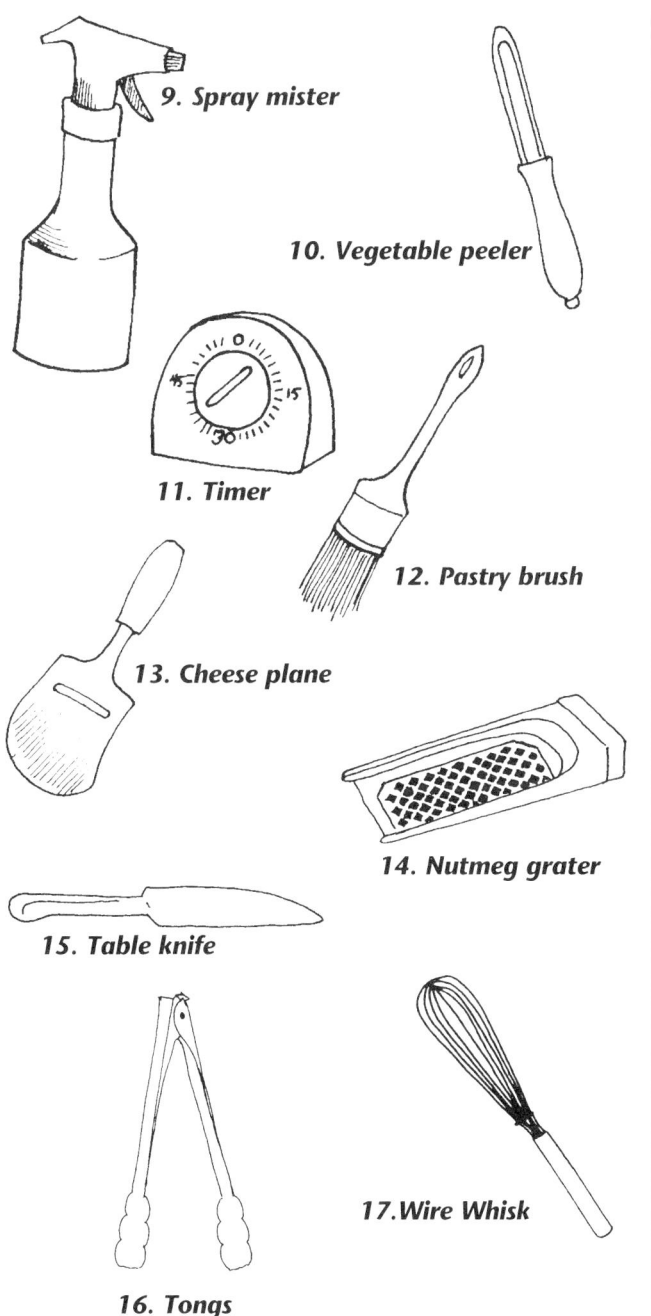

Special Groceries

Listed below are some of my favorite ingredients because they taste great and they don't have any harmful preservatives (chemical additives that are used to prevent the decay of food).

- Classico® spaghetti sauce
- Hain® margarine
- Knudsen® fruit-sweetened preserves
- Fresh whole nutmeg (available in the spice section of most stores)
- Pepperidge Farms® puff pastry
- Canola oil
- Balsamic vinegar
- Roasted carob powder
- Rice paper (available in most Asian stores)
- Yellow fin potatoes
- Verde sauce

FOOD WITHOUT FIRE/ COOKING WITHOUT THE STOVE

Yogurt Cheese

If you like to dip vegetables or crackers, try yogurt cheese. It is healthier than sour cream or cream cheese. You can use it in things like cheesecake, Chili Sundaes, (p. 38) and Righteous Rigatoni, (p. 42). Yogurt cheese is made by removing the whey, which is the liquid part of the yogurt. You can save this liquid and use it soups and stews.

Time: 8 hours   **Serves:** 6

Ready
    6 cup coffee filter (such as Melitta) or plastic funnel with cloth or paper insert
    12 oz. container to hold drained liquid (whey)

Get Set
    1 32 oz. tub of lowfat yogurt
    1/4 teaspoon dill weed
    2 teaspoons mild picante sauce
    1 teaspoon honey
    1 clove minced garlic
    1 tablespoon chopped pimientos
    2 tablespoons minced carrots
    2 tablespoon chopped scallions or green onions
    1/8 teaspoon salt

Go!
1. Place coffee filter on a quart size Tupperware container. Make sure it is steady.

2. Place insert inside coffee filter.

3. Empty yogurt into coffee filter.

4. Cover and let stand overnight.

5. Remove yogurt from filter and put in mixing bowl.

6. Add remaining ingredients and mix together.

TIME OUT/The Story of Yogurt

Desert nomads, who traveled long distances on their camels, accidently discovered yogurt thousands of years ago. They stored their milk supplies in bags made of sheep's stomachs slung over the backs of their animals. The milk was heated by the sun and constantly shaken as the animals walked. Eventually, the milk transformed into a concentrated culture we now call yogurt.

Yogurt received a lot of attention after it cured King Francois I of France in the fourteenth century. He was suffering from an intestinal ailment for which no doctor could find a cure. Finally the sick King heard of a Turkish doctor who had healed many people with a secret fermented milk. He sent for the doctor who told him to eat yogurt every day. When the King recovered he proclaimed yogurt "The milk of eternal life."

Juicy Salad Dressing

This dressing is wonderful for green leaf salads, and you can use it with cold pasta salads, fish, and chicken.

Time: 10 minutes **Serves:** 12

Ready
- large mixing bowl
- whisk
- serrated table knife
- measuring cup

Get Set
- 1/2 cup balsamic vinegar or red vinegar
- 1/4 cup olive oil
- 1/2 cup fresh squeezed orange juice
- 1/2 teaspoon soy sauce
- 2 cloves minced garlic
- 1 chopped scallion
- 1 teaspoon chopped basil (try to get fresh basil)
- 1/2 teaspoon prepared mustard

Go!
1. Combine all ingredients in mixing bowl.
2. Whisk together.
3. Store in refrigerator.

Peeled Salad

This recipe uses an unusual technique to prepare vegetables for salad and it's a lot easier than cutting everything with a knife. One of the vegetables in this recipe is an Asian vegetable called daikon which is nicknamed the "icicle" because of its shape. This tuber is milder than red radishes.

Time: 15 minutes **Serves:** 4

Ready
 vegetable peeler
 salad bowl
 serrated table knife

Get Set
 1 cucumber
 1 carrot
 1/2 daikon radish
 1/2 red bell pepper
 1 chopped scallion
 6 chopped mint leaves
 2 tablespoons juicy salad dressing (see page 16)

Go!
 1. Cut ends off vegetables and peel outer skin off of carrot, daikon, and cucumber.

 In large salad bowl:
 2. Peel cucumber in long strips until you see the seeds.
 3. Peel carrot and daikon completely.
 4. Cut red bell pepper in half, remove seeds and cut into thin strips with table knife.
 5. Slice white portion of scallion into small pieces.
 6. Cut green stems of scallion lengthwise into long strips.
 7. Add chopped mint leaves.
 8. Add 2 tablespoons of fruit dressing.
 9. Toss together.

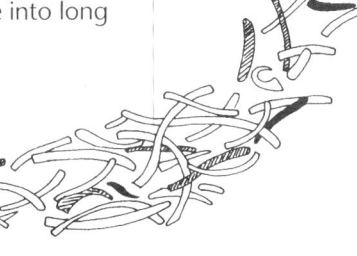

18

Brick Sandwiches

Sandwiches were invented by an Earl named John Montagu who lived in Sandwich, England over 200 years ago. I call this one a brick sandwich. The brick is used to squash the bread once it has been filled with colorful layers of goodies, so please, don't eat the brick!

Time: 20 minutes   **Serves:** 8

Ready
　　table knife
　　1 clean brick (scrub with hot, soapy water, rinse and let dry)
　　aluminum foil
　　plastic wrap

Get Set
　　1 small jar pimientos
　　1/2 sliced avocado
　　1 cup sliced black olives
　　1/4 lb. sliced Swiss cheese
　　1/4 lb. sliced cheddar cheese
　　2 tablespoons chopped red onion
　　small jar mustard
　　small jar low fat mayonnaise
　　1 whole wheat sour dough round loaf of bread

Go!

1. Cut a round circle in the top of the bread around six inches in diameter and set aside.

1.

2. Remove soft inside part of the bread leaving a crust at least 1/2 inch thick.

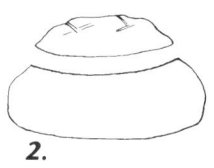
2.

3. Spread mayonnaise on the inside of bread loaf.

4. Arrange olives in a single layer inside the bottom of the bread.

5. Next, add a layer of chopped onions, then sliced cheddar, pimentos strips, sliced avocado, and sliced swiss.

6. Replace top portion of bread.

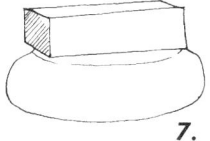
7.

7. Wrap loaf in plastic wrap, place brick wrapped with foil on top of your bread, and store in refrigerator.

8. Let sit for 6 hours.

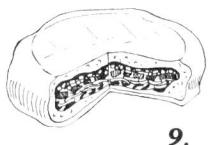
9.

9. Slice bread in half and then into quarters. Then cut quarters into slices one inch thick. Get an adult to help you start.

Sun Burned Tea

Fresh mint is a fun thing to plant because it's so easy to grow. You can buy baby plants from the nursery and plant them in your yard to make tea. Some of the most popular flavors of mint are chocolate, pineapple, peppermint, orange, and strawberry. You can develop a "good nose" by practicing identifying different smells that are used in cooking. Blindfold your friends and see who can correctly identify different kinds of mint.

This recipe has no caffeine so it won't keep you awake after you've gone to bed.

Time: 8 hours   **Serves:** 12

Ready
   1 large gallon glass jar with lid
   hot sunny day

Get Set
   6 bags of Celestial Seasonings™ Tropical Escape Tea (or any tea you like)
   10 fresh mint leaves

Go!
   1. Fill your jar with water.
   2. Add 6 small tea bags and 10 mint leaves.
   3. Put the jar outside in direct sunlight for 8 hours.
   4. Refrigerate.

TIME OUT/The Legend of Tea

Legend has it that over 2,500 years ago an Indian monk named Bodhidharma decided to never sleep again but to spend his nights meditating instead. Even though he was able to stay awake for many days he eventually fell fast asleep. When he woke up he was so disappointed with himself that he buried his face in the ground and began to cry. It was at this place in the ground where the first tea trees grew and as the tea trees grew taller and taller, monkeys were trained to climb them and throw the tea leaves to the ground. It was soon discovered that these leaves helped the monks stay awake because they had a stimulant called caffeine. This stimulant is also found in many cola drinks, such as Coca Cola™.

BLAST OFF IN THE MICROWAVE

Microwaves are actually electromagnetic waves, similar to radio waves. These waves penetrate food and cause its molecules to speed up and vibrate so quickly that they generate heat, which cooks the food. Microwaves vibrate at around 2.5 billion times per second.

Corn Cob Hob Nob

When you cook food in a microwave, you should cover it to keep it from drying out. Corn has it's own natural cover, a husk.

Time: 10 minutes **Serves:** 2

Ready
 1 pair washable gloves

Get Set
 2 ears of corn with husks on
 2 teaspoons margarine

TIME OUT/The Story of Grandfather Corn

Before the days of refrigeration, preserving food was difficult, especially in the summer months. The Sioux Indian Tribe has an interesting story about the gift of corn.

There was an old hermit who lived in the forest all alone for many years, one night while he was asleep, he heard a voice say, "Hermit, I have come to invite you to my home."

For three nights the hermit heard the same voice. He became annoyed and decided to wait up for the voice. As soon as it started to speak, he shot an arrow in its direction and it fell silent.

The next day the hermit ventured out from his tent to find a pile of corn with a trail of kernels leading into the woods. This led him to a mound of earth which he dug up. To his amazement, he found different bags of delicious food, including one with corn that actually had the tip of the arrow he had shot the night before. It was then that the hermit realized he could bury his food in the ground to keep it from spoiling. Although the summer heat could ruin food, the underground temperature kept food cool and it lasted all summer. This secret came to be known as the "Gift of corn."

Go!

1. Blast corn for 3 minutes on high setting.

2. Put on your gloves and turn corn over and blast for 3 more minutes.

3. Let stand for 3 minutes.

4. Put gloves on to peel cooked corn. If you don't have gloves you can use a towel to protect your hands from the heat.

5. Serve with margarine and fresh ground black pepper.

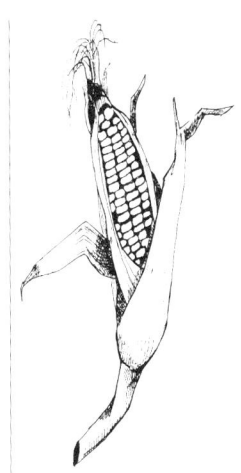

TIME OUT/The Story of Popcorn

People have been eating popcorn for over 5,000 years. The first corn was probably popped when someone accidently put some kernels in a campfire. The explosions must have been pretty scary.

In 1900, a corn show craze started among Midwestern U.S. farmers. They competed for prizes for the most perfect ear of corn. These contests were judged in corn palaces actually built out of corn. There is still one in Mitchell, South Dakota, built in 1921 from 2,000 bushels of colorful corn.

Spectacular Spud Bar

There are over 300 varieties of potatoes in the world today and many of them have interesting colors. Some of my favorites are the yellow fin potato and the Peruvian purple potato.

Time: 20 minutes **Serves:** 4

Ready
   oven mitts
   fork

Get Set
   2 Russet potatoes

   Extra toppings:
   1 chopped scallion
   1/4 cup yogurt cheese
   1/2 cup grated cheese
   2 tablespoons margarine
   1 tablespoon chives
   1/4 cup black olives

Go!
1. Pierce potatoes with fork.

2. Cook in microwave for 12 minutes, 6 on one side and 6 on the other.

3. Let potatoes stand for 3 minutes.

4. With oven mitts on, squeeze potatoes to check to see if they're done. Potatoes should start to collapse when squeezed.

5. Arrange extra toppings in small bowls on table.

6. Cut potatoes in half and add the extra toppings you like.

TIME OUT/Potatoes of the Past
One of the great heroes of potato history was a French pharmacist named Auguste Parmentier. He gave a formal dinner for Benjamin Franklin that consisted entirely of potatoes. Parmentier convinced King Louis 16th, who ruled France from 1774-1792, that these vegetables could grow in almost any soil and help feed starving peasants. When Parmentier presented Queen Marie Antoinette with a bouquet of potato blossoms, she liked them so much she wore them in her hair. To this day potato blossoms bloom every year at the grave of Auguste Parmentier.

Potato chips were invented in 1853 by a Indian chef named Chief Crum, at a country club in Sarasota Springs, New York. He became very annoyed when a customer complained that his french fries were too thick. The chef decided to teach his guest a lesson and sliced the potatoes as thinly as he could. The man who complained liked them so much he asked for more! Soon potato chips were served everywhere in Sarasota...and of course now, everywhere in the world.

Blasted Bananas

There are almost 150 varieties of bananas grown throughout the world. Richardsons Seaside Banana Garden, located in Conchito, California, (805-643-4061) has at least 40 varieties they can ship to you, such as Sweet Dwarf, Manzano, Squatter Red, Blue Java, Cardaba, and Brazilian.

Time: 15 minutes   **Serves:** 6

Ready
  table knife
  pastry brush
  oven mitts
  microwave dish with glass lid

Get Set
  6 bananas
  1/2 cup crushed peanuts
  3 tablespoons unsweetened grated coconut

  For spice butter, mix and cook in microwave for 45 seconds:
  1 teaspoon maple syrup
  1 oz. margarine
  1/2 teaspoon carob powder
  pinch of ground cloves

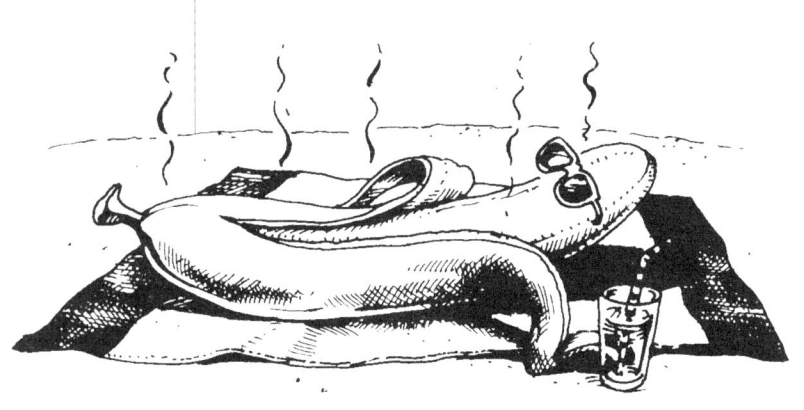

Go!
1. Cut bananas in half lengthwise.

2. Lay bananas in baking dish flat side down.

3. Mix melted margarine and pour over bananas.

4. Sprinkle crushed peanuts and grated coconut over bananas.

5. Bake in microwave for 2 minutes.

 TIME OUT/ The Total Banana
Bananas are a very popular fruit today, rich in potassium and vitamin C. Yet in 1690 the Puritans found them quite unappealing. When the green bananas were harvested they would boil them skins and all! Eventually the Puritans learned how to ripen this fruit and it tasted delicious without the skins. Banana peels have some interesting uses. They can actually shine leather shoes. Use the inside of the peels and wipe clean with cotton cloth. The oil in the skins gives a nice shine if you run out of shoe polish. They are also useful in your garden. Rose bushes love them. Just cut up leftover peels and bury them around your rose bushes (about three peels per plant). The peels give off nutrients that help roses thrive.

Whirlwind Chicken

This dish is fast and easy and perfect for family dinners. This chicken is cooked in what's called a marinade, which is a liquid mixture that helps to make the chicken tender and flavorful. One of the ingredients in this marinade is balsamic vinegar, which is aged in wooden barrels and can take up to ten years to make. Some of these vinegars are older than you are!

Time: 20 minutes   **Serves:** 4

Ready
microwave cooking dish with lid
table knife

Get Set
2 six ounce boneless, skinless, chicken breasts

For Marinade:
3 tablespoons green chili sauce or canned green chilies
juice from 1/2 orange
juice from 1/2 lime
3 minced garlic cloves
1 tablespoon soy sauce
1 tablespoon balsamic vinegar or red wine vinegar

Go!
1. Mix marinade ingredients together in microwave cookware dish 7 x11 inches or larger, and add chicken breast.

2. Turn chicken over a few times and let it sit in the marinade for around 15 minutes.

3. Cover your dish with a glass lid or use microwave wrap and poke a few holes in the top with a fork.

4. Cook for six minutes and let stand for three minutes.

AT HOME ON THE RANGE/ COOKING ON THE STOVE

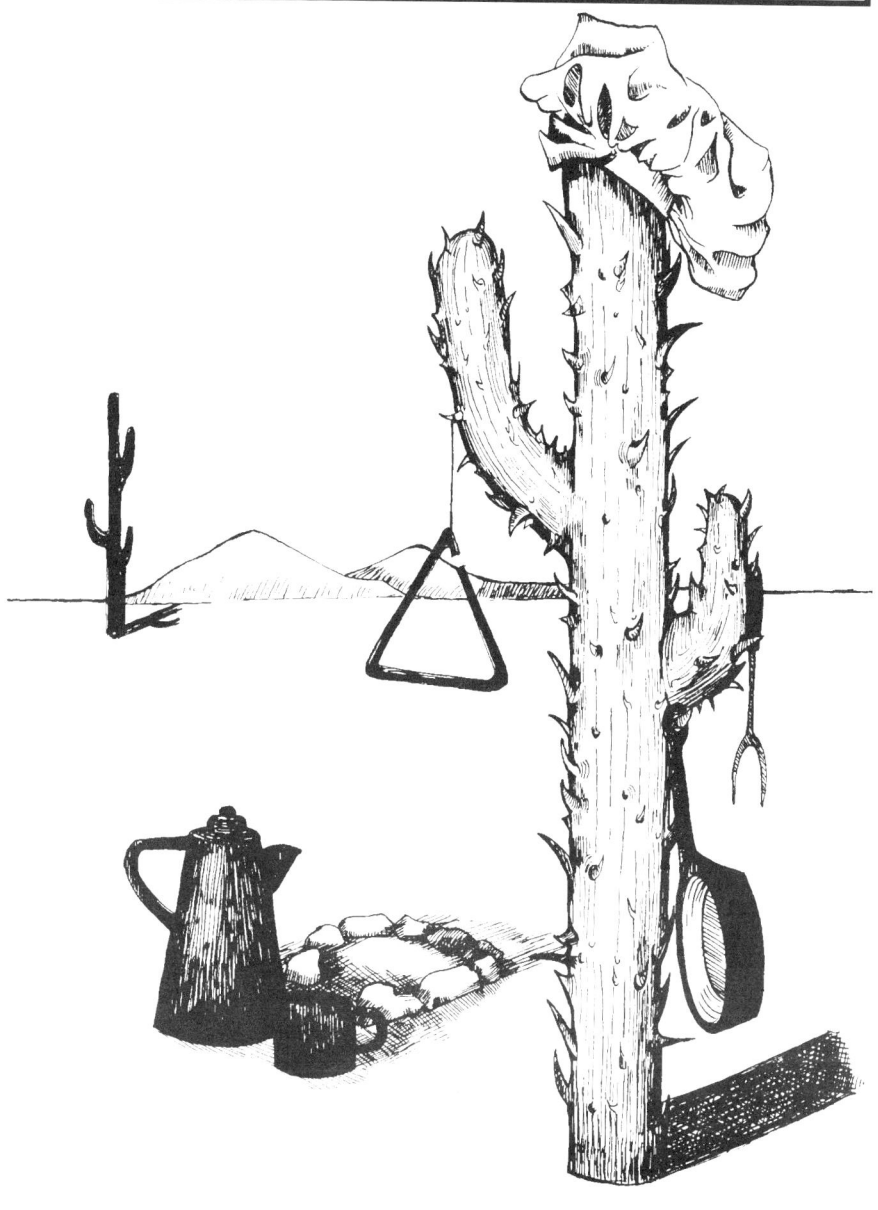

Deviled Eggs

The only thing you need to cut these eggs is a string. It actually cuts them better than a knife. You can also use a plastic baggie instead of a pastry bag. Simply cut off a small 1/2 inch corner from the bottom of the bag and use it just like a pastry bag by filling the bag and squeezing mixture out through hole in bottom.

Time: 15 minutes   **Serves:** 4

Ready
pot for boiling water
colander
one piece of thread
pastry bag with metal tipped end or plastic baggie

Get Set
4 eggs
1 tablespoon low fat mayonnaise.
1/4 teaspoon paprika
1/2 teaspoon pickle juice
1 tablespoon mild picante sauce

Go!

1. Place eggs in pot and fill with cold water until eggs are covered.

2. Once water boils, cook for 5 minutes.

3. Turn heat off and let eggs sit in water for 7 more minutes.

4. Pour eggs and water through colander in sink and rinse with cold water.

5. Crack and peel eggs.

6. Tie a loop around middle part of peeled egg with thread and pull together in a knot. This will cut your egg in half.

7. Drop yolks into bowl and mix with lowfat mayonnaise, pickle juice, and picante sauce.

8. Trim pointed bottoms of egg halves so they will stand up with holes facing upward.

9. Place egg yolk mixture into pastry bag or cut plastic baggie and squeeze into holes of egg whites.

10. Sprinkle one pinch of paprika on top of each egg.

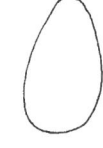
5.

6.

7.

8.

9.

Marbled Eggs

This recipe can be lots of fun and less messy than using dye to color eggs. Once you've soaked these eggs overnight they will look like marble after they're peeled. You could also use other strong colors such as tea or beet juice.

Time: 12 hours **Serves:** 4

Ready
   small boiling pot

Get Set
   4 hard boiled eggs
   1 pint red raspberry juice concentrate

Go!
   1. Crack eggs completely but do not peel.

   2. Place in juice concentrate so eggs are covered.

   3. Soak overnight.

   4. Peel and rinse.

TIME OUT/Centrifugal Force
Take a raw egg and a hard boiled egg and try this experiment. Carefully spin the egg on a flat surface and stop it with your finger. Quickly lift your finger. The cooked egg stands still and the raw egg continues to spin. What causes this? The yolk of the egg is still spinning!

Lava Sauce

There are lots of good pasta sauces that you can buy and take one step further with some additional ingredients. One of my favorites is Classico Spicy Red Pepper Sauce. You can use any tomato sauce you like. This sauce is great on spaghetti and pizza.

Time: 15 minutes   **Serves:** 4

Ready
- cooking pot
- wooden spoon
- rotary grater
- table knife
- garlic press

Get Set
- 1 32 oz. jar of Classico® Spicy Red Pepper Sauce
- 1 grated zucchini
- 1 peeled, grated carrot (cut off stem)
- 2 cloves minced garlic

Go!
1. Place sauce in pot on stove.

2. Add all ingredients to sauce.

3. Cook over low heat, for ten minutes, stirring frequently.

Runaway Fillet

The secret to this recipe is the fresh nutmeg. Even though you can buy this spice already ground, grating whole nutmeg makes a tremendous difference!

Time: 20 minutes   **Serves:** 4

Ready
    small casserole dish
    pastry brush
    spice grater
    oven mitts

Get Set
    1/4 cup margarine
    1 pound of fresh sole or other fish fillet
    1/4 cup crushed slivered almonds
    1/2 cup whole wheat bread crumbs

Seasonings:
    1 teaspoon freshly grated nutmeg
    2 tablespoons onion flakes
    2 teaspoons Italian seasoning
    1/4 teaspoon salt
    1/2 teaspoon garlic powder
    1 tablespoon hulled sesame seeds

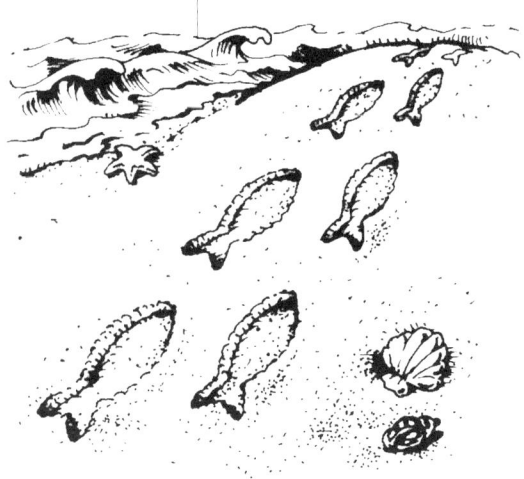

Go!
1. Add seasonings to bread crumbs.

2. Pre-heat oven for 10 minutes at 350 degrees.

3. Place fish fillets in baking dish and brush lightly with margarine.

4. Sprinkle bread crumbs over top of fish until lightly covered.

5. Lightly pat margarine over bread crumbs with pastry brush.

6. Bake for 10 minutes.

7. Remove from oven using oven mitts.

8. Turn oven off.

Asparagus Tepees

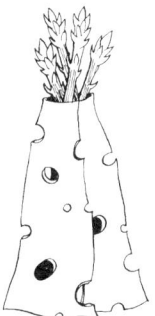

Time: 15 minutes   **Serves:** 3

Ready
  1 large pot
  table knife
  colander
  tongs
  large container of ice water
  cheese plane

Get Set
  one bunch of asparagus
  1/4 pound sliced Swiss cheese
  1/4 cup of your favorite dip

Go!

  1. Cut off tough ends of asparagus (around one to two inches).

  2. Bring pot of water to a boil.

  3. Carefully place asparagus into boiling water for 45 seconds.

  4. Drain in colander in sink.

  5. Place in ice water for 2 minutes and drain.

  6. Cut round 1/2 inch slice of cucumber and lay flat.

  7. Cut a circle inside cucumber slice so it looks like a doughnut.

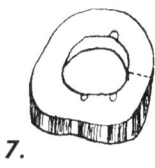

8. Place tips of asparagus inside round of cucumber so it circles just below tips of asparagus.

9. Stand pieces up with flowers pointing upward and pull bottom of each asparagus outward to form circle at bottom of tepee.

10. Slice pieces of Swiss cheese with cheese plane and wrap around tepee of asparagus until only the green tips are showing.

11. Serve with your favorite dip.

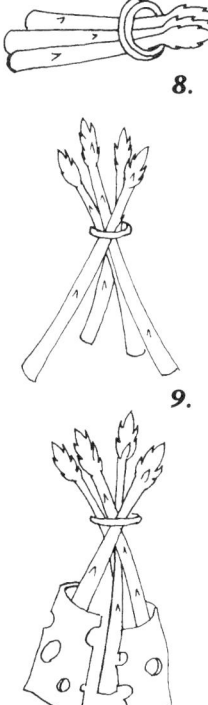

Chili Sundaes

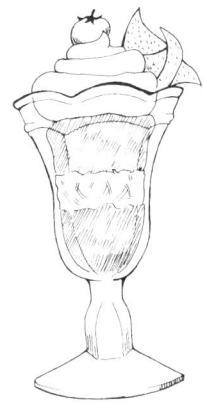

Time: 15 minutes   **Serves:** 4

Ready
  4 sundae glasses or tall clear glasses with wide mouths
  small pot
  wooden spoon
  pastry bag with fluted end

Get Set
  8 tortilla chips
  1 can chili (you can use vegetarian)
  1/2 pound cheddar cheese
  1 cup yogurt cheese (see page 14)
  1/2 cup pecan pieces
  4 cherry tomatoes

Go!

1. Open can of chili, pour into pot and heat over low flame, stirring with wooden spoon.

2. Grate cheese with rotary grater.

3. Fill sundae glass 1/4 full with heated chili.

4. Add layer of grated cheese.

5. Add more chili until glass is 3/4 full.

6. Fill pastry bag with yogurt cheese and squeeze circles into top of glass.

7. Place cherry tomato on top of yogurt cheese.

8. Sprinkle pecan pieces over yogurt and garnish with chips.

Noodle Twister

Time: 25 minutes   **Serves:** 6

Ready
- large pot
- mixing bowl
- table knife
- wooden spoon

Get Set
- 1/4 cup juicy salad dressing (see page 16)
- 1/4 cup mild picante sauce
- 1 jar marinated quartered artichoke hearts
- 3 cups spiral pasta (Rotelle)
- 1 cup frozen peas, thawed for 10 minutes
- 1 tablespoon Parmesan cheese
- 2 tablespoons walnut pieces
- 1 chopped red bell pepper

Go!
1. Bring one quart of water to a boil in cooking pot.
2. Add pasta and boil for 12 minutes, stirring occasionally.
3. Drain pasta in colander in sink.
4. Rinse in cold water and let drain for 5 minutes.
5. Put cool pasta in mixing bowl and add remaining ingredients.
6. Gently mix together and refrigerate.

40

Fiesta Pie

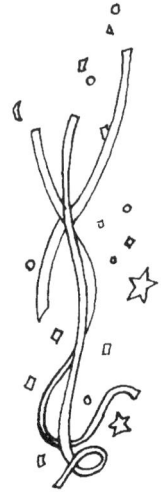

This recipe is like cornbread, but because it's cooked at a lower temperature the texture gets chewy and firm.

Time: 45 minutes   **Serves:** 12

Ready
    small casserole dish
    oven mitts
    2 large mixing bowls
    wooden mixing spoon
    flour sifter

Get Set
Dry Ingredients:
1 chopped green bell pepper
1 chopped red bell pepper
3 chopped scallions
1 cup sifted cornmeal
1 cup sifted unbleached flour
1/2 teaspoon salt
2 teaspoons baking powder
1/3 cup Parmesan cheese
1 tablespoon chili powder
1/8 teaspoon cayenne

Wet Ingredients:
2 minced garlic cloves
1 cup skim milk
1 egg
1/4 cup oil

Go!
1. Pre-heat oven to 350 degrees.

2. Sift cornmeal, flour, and baking powder in large mixing bowl.

3. Add peppers and scallions to bowl.

4. Add remaining dry ingredients and stir together.

5. Separately mix wet ingredients in another mixing bowl.

6. Pour wet ingredients into dry ingredients and mix together.

7. Pour one teaspoon of oil into baking dish and smear so it coats inside of baking dish. Pour contents of bowl into baking dish.

8. Bake for 35 minutes at 350 degrees.

9. Remove from oven with oven mitts and turn oven off.

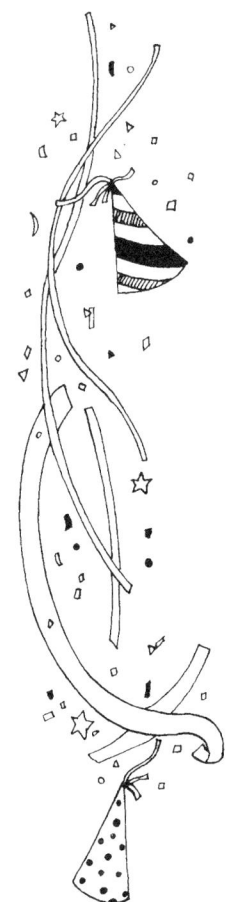

Righteous Rigatoni

This recipe is a good example of what many people call "finger food": easy for friends to enjoy at a party.

Time: 30 minutes　　　　　　　　**Serves:** 6

Ready
　　boiling pot
　　tongs or slotted spoon
　　colander

Get Set
　　1/2 pound small fresh green beans with stems removed
　　1/2 cup yogurt cheese (see page 14)
　　1/2 cup dry rigatoni noodles

Go!

1. Bring one quart of water to a boil.

2. Boil green beans in water for 2 minutes and turn heat off.

3. Remove green beans with tongs or slotted spoon.

4. Rinse in cold water.

5. Turn flame back on and bring water to a boil again.

6. Add 1/4 teaspoon salt to cooking pot.

7. Add pasta and cook for 15 minutes, stirring frequently.

8. Drain in colander in sink.

9. Rinse with cold water, drain and let cool.

10. Push green bean inside rigatoni pasta.

11. Dip in yogurt cheese.

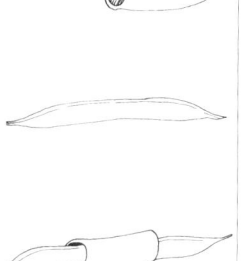

10.

BECOMING A FOOD AMBASSADOR/ INTERNATIONAL RECIPES

"If you want to understand another culture then find out about their food."

Jeff Smith

The world is filled with unique and interesting people and you're one of them! There are great things we can learn from each other. When you cook food from other countries you will discover a lot of new ingredients that may help you learn about other countries.

Spring Rolls from Viet Nam

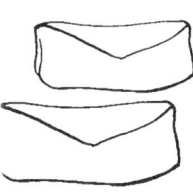

These are shaped just like egg rolls, but are not fried. To eat, pick up rolls with your fingers and dip into soy sauce.

Time: 30 minutes   **Makes:** 4 rolls

Ready
  spray mister bottle
  small mixing bowl

Get Set
  For Spring Rolls:
  quartered rice paper (available in Asian stores already cut)
  1 peeled cucumber
  8 boiled shelled shrimp
  4 green scallion strips 3 inches long
  1/3 peeled daikon radish
  8 fresh mint leaves broken in small pieces
  1/4 cup soy sauce

Go!

1. Bring one pint of water in a small pot to a boil.

2. Add shrimp and cook for 3 minutes.

3. Drain shrimp in colander in sink and rinse in cold water.

4. Peel shrimp and cut into bite size pieces.

5. Peel 8 cucumber strips and 8 daikon strips with vegetable peeler.

6. Lay out rice paper with point facing upward.

7. Spray lightly with mister bottle.

8. Wait one minute for paper to soften.

9. Place 2 cut shrimp in center of each paper.

10. Lay 2 strips each of cucumber, daikon, and scallion stems on top of shrimp.

11. Fold sides inward and roll up from bottom.

12. Serve with soy sauce.

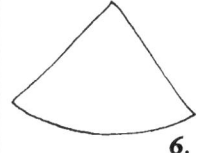

6.

7.

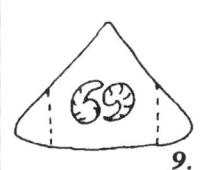

9.

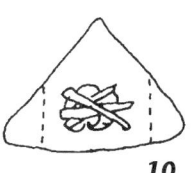

10.

11.

Spaghetti Frittata From Italy

Italy

If you like macaroni and cheese you'll love this recipe. And besides, frittatas are an excellent way to use up leftovers, especially spaghetti.

Time: 40 minutes   **Serves:** 12

Ready
- small casserole dish
- mixing bowl
- whisk
- oven mitts

Get Set
- 6 fresh eggs
- 1 cup grated Swiss cheese
- 1 cup grated cheddar
- 1/2 cup feta cheese
- 3 cups of leftover spaghetti in its own sauce
- 3 pinches of salt and pepper

Go!
1. Crack six eggs in a mixing bowl and whisk together.

2. Add leftovers and grated cheese.

3. Coat the inside of casserole dish with 1 teaspoon vegetable oil.

4. Pour mixture from bowl into baking dish.

5. Cover with microwave wrap and punch a few holes in top.

6. Microwave for 15 minutes and let stand for 5 minutes.

7. Turn on the oven to broil and pre-heat 5 minutes.

8. Remove dish from microwave and remove plastic wrap.

9. Place baking dish in the broiler for three minutes or until it turns golden brown.

10. Remove with oven mitts and let cool for 5 minutes.

11. Cut into squares with tableknife and remove with spatula.

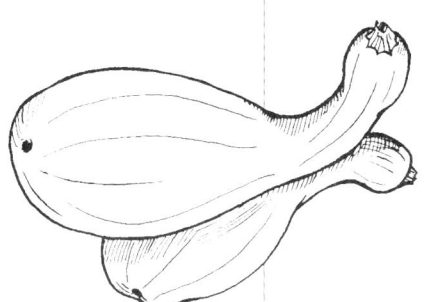

Checkered Quesadillas From Mexico

Time: 15 minutes **Serves:** 4

Ready
- pizza cutter
- rotary grater
- pastry brush
- table knife

Get Set
- 2 white and 2 whole wheat tortillas
- 1/2 cup Monterey Jack cheese
- 1/2 sliced fresh papaya
- 2 tablespoons hot sauce
- 1/2 sliced avocado
- olive oil

For each checkered tortilla use these amounts:
- 2 handfuls of grated cheese
- 3-4 papaya slices
- 3-4 avocado slices
- 1 tablespoon green chili sauce or mild picante sauce

Go!

1. Take one white and one whole wheat tortilla that are the same size and cut each in 7 strips, using pizza cutter or table knife.

2. Smear small amount of oil on baking sheet.

3. Assemble checkered tortillas on baking sheet by replacing every white strip with a whole wheat strip. Braid pieces together.

4. Layer grated cheese on top of checkered tortillas.

5. Add slices of avocado and papaya.

6. Top with hot sauce and more grated cheese.

7. Place plain whole tortillas on top of stuffing.

8. Brush with olive oil.

9. Bake for 7 minutes.

10. Remove with oven mitts and let cool for 2 minutes.

11. Flip quesadillas over with spatula so checkered side faces up.

12. Cut in wedges with pizza cutter.

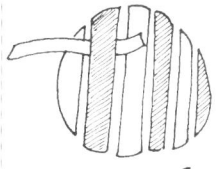

1.

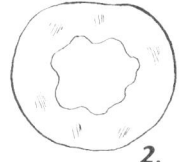

2.

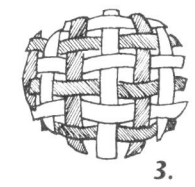

3.

Spice Island Muffins From Indonesia

If you bite an unpeeled orange it tastes bitter, but small amounts of grated orange peel in baking are delicious. This is called orange zest. Remember to grate only the outside part of the peel.

Time: 45 minutes   **Serves:** 16

Ready
muffin pans
paper or foil baking cups
mixing spoon
2 large mixing bowls

Get Set
Mix wet ingredients:
2 very ripe bananas
1 8 oz. can crushed pineapple
1/2 cup honey
2 eggs
1/3 cup canola oil or other vegetable oil
grated orange peel from one orange
fresh juice of two oranges
1 teaspoon baking powder dissolved in 1 tablespoon water
    1 cup grated carrots
        1 cup grated zucchini

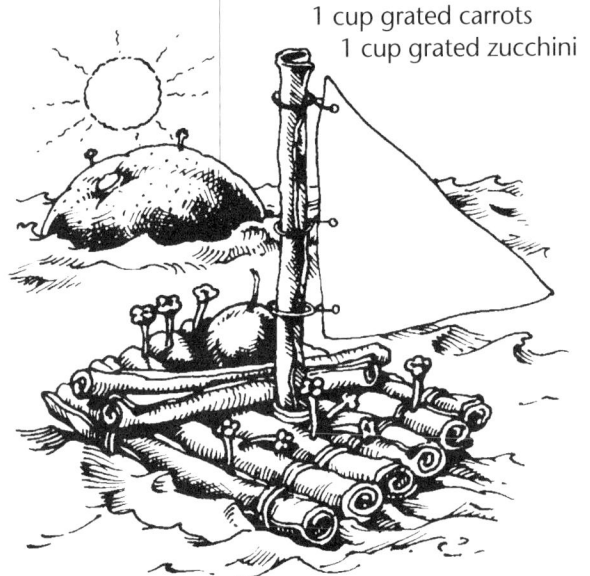

Separately mix dry ingredients:

2 1/4 cups sifted whole wheat pastry flour
2 1/4 cups sifted unbleached white flour
1 teaspoon sifted baking soda
1/2 teaspoon cinnamon
1/4 teaspoon freshly grated nutmeg
1/4 teaspoon ground cloves
3 tablespoons chopped pecans
2 tablespoons shredded unsweetened coconut
1/2 cup raisins
2 tablespoons sesame seeds (save 1 additional tablespoon of seeds to sprinkle on top of muffins for decoration)

Go!

1. Mix wet ingredients in a bowl.

2. Mix dry ingredients in a separate bowl.

3. Pour wet mixture into dry ingredients and mix. It's okay to leave some lumps.

4. Spoon into muffin tins and lightly sprinkle sesame seeds on top of muffins.

5. Bake at 350 degrees for 30 minutes.

6. Remove with oven mitts and let cool for 10 minutes.

TIME OUT/The Origin of Cloves

Cloves originally came from the tropical islands of Indonesia. These tiny volcanic islands, in the South Pacific, were sought after for their precious wealth of pepper, cinnamon, nutmeg and cloves.

In ancient Chinese courts, people were required to put cloves in their mouths so their breath would not offend the emperor.

Triangles of Egypt

Pita bread, often called flat bread, comes from the Middle East. It is flat because it has no yeast and doesn't rise like other bread. For more about yeast, see chapter 6, on Dessert Chemistry.

Time: 10 minutes **Serves:** 4

Ready
large baking sheet
pastry brush
small cooking pot
garlic press

Get Set
Three six inch whole wheat pita rounds

Mix together in small cooking pot:
2 tablespoons margarine
1 1/2 teaspoons lemon juice
1 minced clove garlic
pinch salt
1/8 teaspoon cayenne
1 tablespoon minced fresh parsley (you can pinch it with your fingers)

Go!

1. Separate each pita round into two pieces and cut into triangles.

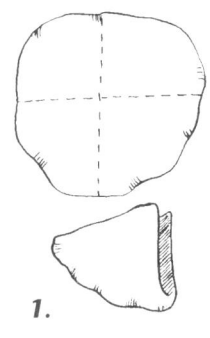
1.

2. Heat liquid mixture over low flame on stove for 5 minutes.

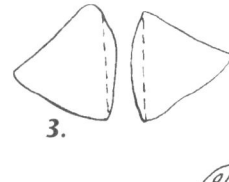
3.

3. Lay out pita triangles on baking sheet so pieces are spaced apart.

4.

4. Brush triangles lightly with the liquid mixture.

5. Bake at 350 degrees for 10 minutes.

EDIBLE ART/ BEAUTIFUL FOOD YOU CAN EAT

Spooky Hobgoblins

Time: 15 minutes   **Serves:** 2

Ready
- can opener
- pot for boiling water
- vegetable peeler
- salad plate

Get Set
one small can each of:
- pineapple rings
- Mandarin oranges
- peach halves
- 1 batch green hair scallions (see recipe, page 55)
- 1 marbled egg (see recipe, page 32) or use kiwi fruit
- 2 carrot turbans (see recipe, page 56)
- 3 cloves
- 1 head of curly leaf lettuce

Go!

1. Refrigerate canned fruit one hour before opening.

2. Open cans and drain juice.

3. Rinse three leaves of lettuce and overlap on salad plate.

4. Place peach half in the middle of lettuce for body.

5. Break circles of pineapple in half and use as arms.

6. Use carrot turbans for hands.

7. Use mandarin orange segments for feet.

8. Use marbled egg for head or use 1 slice of peeled kiwi fruit.

9. Put green hair scallion curls on top of egg.

55

Green Haired Scallion

Used In Hobgoblins

Time: 10 minutes   **Serves:** 2

Ready
    serrated table knife
    small bowl of ice water

Get Set
    one scallion

Go!

1. Cut the scallion where the white part meets the green stems.

2. Wrap up white portion and refrigerate for another recipe.

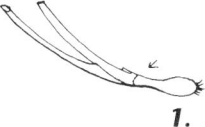

1.

3. Slice green stems in thin strips lengthwise. You should be able to get at least four separate strips out of one stem.

4. Put in bowl of ice water for 5 minutes.

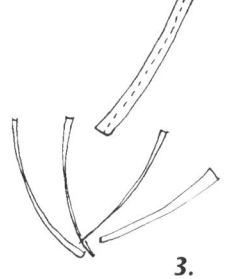

3.

4.

56

Carrot Turbans

Used In Hobgoblins

Time: 10 minutes   **Serves:** 4

Ready
vegetable peeler
toothpicks
small bowl of ice water
serrated table knife

Get Set
1 medium sized carrot

Go!

1. Peel the carrot.

2. Cut off both ends.

1.

3. Cut carrot in half lengthwise and lay flat side up.

3.

4. Hold small end of one half and peel one long slice from flat side of carrot.

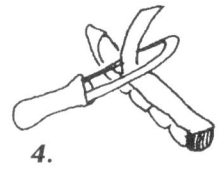
4.

5. Roll sliced carrot up and push toothpick through it.

6. Put in ice water for ten minutes.

7. Remove toothpick when ready to use.

5.

Shrunken Heads

This is a good example of a dried food. For centuries dried foods were the only way to survive on long voyages and journeys, because they required no refrigeration and were very lightweight. This particular dried food makes a great gag for Halloween.

Time: 2 weeks

Ready
table knife
string
vegetable peeler

Get Set
1 large apple

Go!
1. Peel an apple with vegetable peeler and leave stem in place.

2. Carve a large face in the apple with the tip of the vegetable peeler.

3. Tie string on the stem and hang it in a warm, dry place for one or two weeks.

4. Hang in your doorway for Halloween.

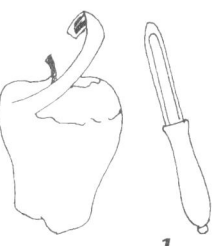

1.

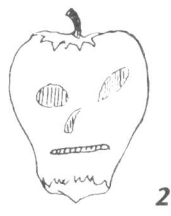

2.

Undercover Shrimp Boat with Red Handed Sauce

Time: 30 minutes   **Serves:** 4

Ready
- table knife
- vegetable peeler
- small pot
- colander
- wooden skewer
- small mixing bowl
- melon baller

Get Set
- 1 bag shrimp boil
- 3 slices of firm cheese
- 3 thin celery sticks
- 3 cherry tomatoes
- 1 pound medium sized shrimp
- 1 cucumber

For Red Handed Sauce Mix:
- juice of 1 lemon (strain seeds)
- 2 tablespoons ketchup
- 2 tablespoons horseradish
- 2 tablespoons hot sauce
- 1 dash Worcestershire sauce

Go!

1. Peel cucumber and carve a hollowed out opening with melon baller to hold sauce.

2. Fill inside of cucumber halfway with sauce.

3. Bring 1 quart of water to a boil on stove in small cooking pot.

4. Add bag of shrimp boil and squeezed lemon peel used for sauce.

5. Let water boil for 3 minutes.

6. Add shrimp and cook for 4 minutes.

7. Drain in colander and rinse in cold water.

8. Save bag of shrimp boil and freeze for another recipe.

9. Peel shrimp and hang over sides of cucumber with tails on the outside.

10. Stick wooden skewer through sliced cheese and hoist into center of cucumber boat.

11. Top with flag made out of leftover foil.

12. Place cherry tomatoes inside boat.

13. Lay celery sticks in between shrimp for paddles.

Radish Mouse

Time: 10 minutes   **Serves:** 2

Ready
  serrated table knife

Get Set
  2 red radishes

Go!

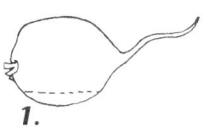

1. Take a single radish and slice off a small sliver from bottom.

2. Lay radish on flat side.

3. Cut this small piece in half lengthwise. These pieces will be your ears.

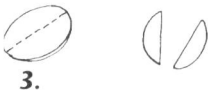

4. Carve two small holes above the root. These will be your eyes.

5. Work your radish pieces into the holes with the white part facing forward.

Radish Jacks

Time: 5 minutes   **Serves:** 2

Ready
serrated table knife

Get Set
2 red radishes

Go!

1. Cut two thin slices of radish.

2. Cut one line from the center to the edge on two thin pieces.

3. Carefully fit the two pieces together.

TIME OUT/The Story of the Jack o' Lantern

Once upon a time there was a stingy, clever man named Jack who was a terrible liar. Jack was so clever that he even tricked the devil into promising that he would never ask for Jack's soul. When Jack died he was refused entry into heaven because he had led such a dishonest life. However, when he tried to enter the gates of Hades, the Devil also refused him, because he feared Jack would trick him again. "At least give me a light to find my way," Jack pleaded. So the Devil tossed him a burning coal. Jack took it and placed it inside a turnip he was eating at the time and the first Jack o' Lantern was born. To this day it is said that Jack still roams the earth with his lantern on Halloween.

Pastamobile

Some designs with food are meant to be eaten right away, while others are only for decoration. With this recipe you could reuse the pasta or make it more permanent by gluing it together.

Time: 20 minutes

Ready
worktable

Get Set
Start collecting different varieties of dried pasta, such as wagon wheels, rigatoni, large and small shells, bowties, lasagna and spaghetti.

Go!

1. Make wheel axles with spaghetti and wagon wheels.

2. Use lasagna for flat bed cargo bay.

3. Build passenger cab with rigatoni.

4. Use shells for bumpers.

5. Use glue if you want to keep your pastamobile.

6. Balance pasta carefully without using glue if you want to eat it!

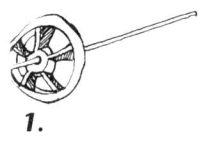
1.

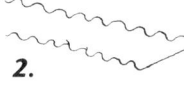
2.

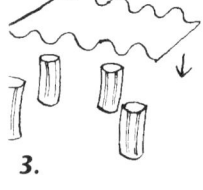
3.

4.

Cucumber Flowers

This is a very practical garnish because you can put a lot of things inside it. Can you think of anything that would make the cucumber look more like a flower?

Time: 10 minutes　　　　　　　　**Serves:** 3

Ready
　　serrated tableknife

Get Set
　　1 cucumber (buy it unwaxed if you can)

Go!
1. Cut off the ends of cucumber.

2. Cut cucumber three ways at 45 degrees.

3. Slowly pull pieces apart.

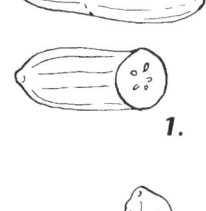

1.

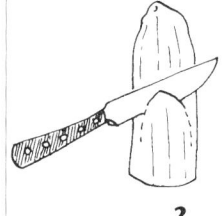

2.

3.

Captured Green Beans in a Cucumber Chain

Time: 20 minutes   **Serves:** 3

Ready
    small pot
    circular cutter
    colander

Get Set
    1/2 pound fresh green beans
    1 unwaxed cucumber

Go!

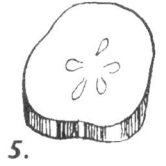

1. Bring 2 cups of water to a boil.

2. Break stems off green beans.

3. Put beans in boiling water for two minutes.

4. Drain in colander and rinse with cold water.

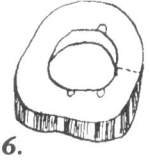

5. Cut 3 cucumber rounds 1/2 inch thick.

6. Remove inside seeds with table knife or small circular cutter.

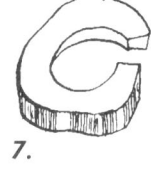

7. Cut one slit in one of the cucumber rounds.

8. Fill uncut cucumber round with green beans.

9. Link remaining two rounds together.

Designer Beans

Time: 24 hours

Ready
small bowl
toothpicks

Get Set
1/2 cup of your favorite beans

Go!
1. Cover beans with water and soak beans in a bowl overnight.

2. Use toothpicks and gently stick them into the sides of your beans.

3. Design bean structures of anything you can imagine.

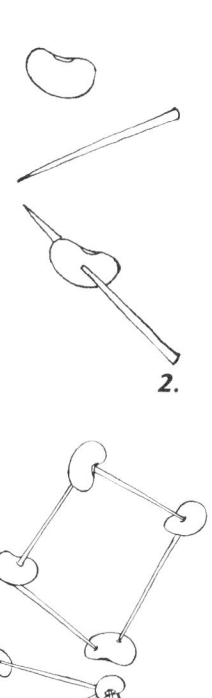

Fruit Flag Pizza

Time: 30 minutes **Serves:** 14

For Cookie Dough:
Ready
- mixing bowl
- electric beater or wire whisk
- flour sifter
- spatula

Get Set
- 1/4 cup honey
- 1 egg
- 1/4 cup margarine
- 2 tablespoons frozen pineapple concentrate
- 2 tablespoons vanilla yogurt
- 1 cup granola
- 1/2 cup unbleached flour
- 1/4 teaspoon baking powder
- 1/4 teaspoon baking soda
- 1/4 teaspoon salt

Go!

1. Mix honey and egg together in mixing bowl, using wire whisk or electric beater.

2. Add margarine, pineapple concentrate, yogurt, and granola.

3. Sift in remaining dry ingredients and mix into batter.

4. Smear thin layer of vegetable oil over baking sheet.

5. Spread cookie batter out in one thin rectangular flag shape.

6. Bake in oven for 12 minutes at 350 degrees.

For Fruit Flag Topping:
Ready
> 1 cup plain yogurt cheese with no seasoning added (see recipe p. 14)
> small mixing bowl
> spatula
> colander

Get Set
> 1 pint blueberries
> 1 pint strawberries
> 1 kiwi fruit

Go!
1. Spread thin layer of yogurt cheese on baked cookie dough.

2. Peel kiwi fruit and place 1 slice in upper left hand corner.

3. Rinse strawberries and slice in half to design red stripes.

4. Rinse blueberries and form blue stripes in between strawberries.

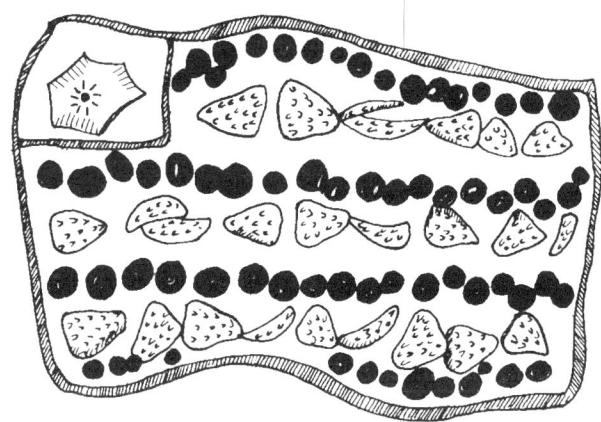

Porcupine Pears

Time: 10 minutes **Serves:** 2

Ready
 table knife

Get Set
 1 tablespoon slivered almonds
 1 can refrigerated pear halves
 small wedge cheddar cheese
 1 strawberry

Go!

1. Place 2 pear halves on flat side in center of plate.

2. Pierce slivered almonds into back of pears so that they stand up.

3. Cut strawberry in half and place one piece at small side of pear for a head.

4. Cut long piece of cheese for tail.

TIME OUT/The Invention of Peanut Butter

In 1890 in Battle Creek, Michigan, Dr. John Kellogg (who became famous for his breakfast cereals), had an assistant who burned a batch of peanuts. Kellogg scolded him for doing so, and the assistant smashed them in anger. The assistant found to his surprize that they had an nice taste and texture. When Dr. Kellogg sampled the smashed peanuts he decided to start selling them and they were an instant success!

Banana Fingers with Peanut Sauce

Ready
  small bowl
  wash hands

Get Set
  2 firm bananas

  For peanut sauce mix:
  2 tablespoons chunky peanut butter
  dash cinnamon

Go!

1. Peel bananas.

2. Hold first banana in one hand.

3. Slowly push your fingers into either end of the banana and it will begin to separate.

3.

4. Remove 1/3 of the banana by moving your finger completely down the length of the banana.

5. Take larger part of the same banana and slowly push your finger into the end of the banana and it will split in half. You should now have three even pieces from one banana.

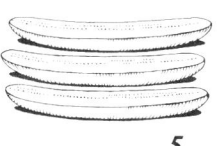
5.

6. Take the second banana and remove 1/3 of it, just like you did with the first banana and set it aside.

7. Take the large portion of the second banana, fill it with peanut butter and sprinkle with cinnamon.

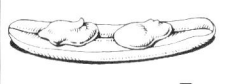
7.

8. Lay two pieces across banana boat for paddles.

9. Break off two pointed ends of remaining banana piece and place behind paddles to make banana people.

9.

Sea Creatures

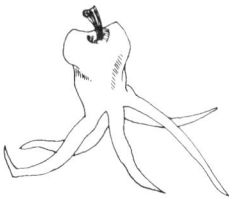

Serving food attractively is an important part of being a good cook. This chili pepper decoration is made with a mild sweet banana pepper that's in the produce section of most stores. Use it with your undercover shrimp boat. (p. 58).

Time: 12 hours

Ready
serrated table knife
container of ice water

Get Set
1 sweet banana pepper or other long chili

Go!
1. Take chili pepper and cut into four quarters, leaving one inch of the stem side uncut.

2. Remove seeds.

3. Put pepper in ice water and refrigerate and it will curl overnight.

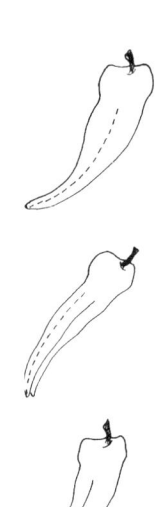

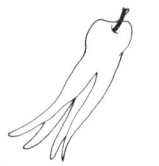

1.

DESSERT CHEMISTRY

Have you ever wondered what makes dough rise? It's usually the active yeast that produces a gas called carbon dioxide. As this gas expands it creates tiny air pockets throughout the dough to give it a light, fluffy texture. To activate yeast you have to "feed it" with sugar and warm water. In this recipe the puff pastry dough has already been made with yeast, so it won't take very long to make.

Pineapple Upside Down Cake

Many cakes, including this one, use baking powder to make the dough rise. Baking powder was invented in Boston in 1853 and is made up of cream of tartar, bicarbonate of soda, and salt. If you want to conduct an experiment to test your baking powder, mix 1 teaspoon of baking powder with 1/3 cup of hot water. Your mixture should start to bubble immediately. Just like in a mixture of activated yeast, these bubbles also give off carbon dioxide gas.

Time: 30 minutes   **Serves:** 4

Ready
Sprinkle a pinch of flour inside 6 oz. custard cups.
whisk
mixing bowl

Get Set
Pre-heat oven to 350 degrees
2 tablespoons honey
1/4 cup margarine, softened
1 egg
1 teaspoon vanilla extract
1/4 cup unsweetened pineapple juice concentrate **plus** 1/4 cup water
1 cup unbleached white flour
1/2 teaspoon baking soda
1/2 teaspoon double acting baking powder

For the Glazed Topping:
1 8 oz. can pineapple rings, unsweetened
maple syrup
margarine
dash of cinnamon

Go!

1. Combine margarine, honey, and egg in mixing bowl and beat together with wire whisk until creamy.

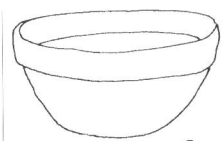

2. Add vanilla extract and pineapple juice.

3. Sift in flour, baking powder, and baking soda and mix together for two minutes.

4. Separately add 1 teaspoon margarine and 2 teaspoons maple syrup to each custard cup and mix together.

5. Blast in microwave for two minutes.

6. Remove from microwave and sprinkle a dash of cinnamon in each cup.

7. Place pineapple ring in the bottom and pour the batter on top, filling cup halfway.

8. Bake for 10-15 minutes at 350 degrees and remove from oven.

9. Loosen the sides of the cakes with thin metal spatula or table knife to keep from sticking.

10. Using oven mitts, turn pan upside down to remove cakes.

11. Let cool for 5 minutes.

Coo-Coo for Coconut

This dessert features a grain called couscous which is easy to work with because it cooks so quickly. It's actually precooked semolina made from wheat and is very popular in North Africa. You can find it in a packaged box or in the bulk section of grocery stores or health stores.

Time: 20 minutes **Serves:** 6

Ready
- medium sized cooking pot
- ceramic, glass or stainless steel pie pan

Get Set
- 1 cup uncooked couscous
- 1 cup chopped apples
- 1 tablespoon margarine
- 1 1/2 cup apple juice
- 1/4 cup honey
- 1/2 teaspoon cinnamon
- 1/2 cup chopped pecans pieces
- 1/4 teaspoon freshly grated nutmeg
- 1/4 cup chopped dates
- juice from 1/2 lemon
- juice from 1/2 orange
- 2 tablespoons dried coconut

Go!
1. Melt margarine in saucepan over low heat and cook apple pieces for 5 minutes.

2. Pour in apple juice and stir.

3. Add remaining ingredients except for couscous and cook over low heat for 5 minutes.

4. Add couscous and cook over medium heat for 3 minutes until most of the liquid is evaporated.

5. Remove from stove and spoon into pie pan.

6. Top with fruit sweetened plum preserves and fresh fruit.

Ginger Bread with Lemon Sauce

In many recipes, baking powder and baking soda are used together. The chemical name for baking soda is sodium bicarbonate. Baking soda can be used to brush your teeth if you run out of toothpaste. It can also be used as a deodorant in the refrigerator to absorb food odors.

Time: 45 minutes   **Serves:** 12

Ready
　　whisk
　　large mixing bowl
　　wooden spoon
　　small pot
　　grater

Get Set
　　1/3 cup margarine
　　1/2 cup maple syrup
　　1 egg
　　1/3 cup light molasses
　　2/3 cup plain yogurt
　　2 cup unbleached flour
　　2 teaspoons double acting baking powder
　　1/4 teaspoon baking soda
　　1 1/4 teaspoon ground ginger
　　1 teaspoon ground cinnamon
　　1/2 teaspoon ground cloves
　　1/2 teaspoon salt

Go!
1. Whisk margarine, molasses and maple syrup together in mixing bowl.

2. Whisk egg and yogurt into mixture.

3. Add sifted flour and mix in the rest of the dry ingredients.

4. Coat baking dish with 1/2 teaspoon oil.

5. Lightly sprinkle bottom of pan with 1 teaspoon flour.

6. Pour batter into pan and smooth edges out with spatula.

7. Bake at 350 degrees for 25 minutes.

For lemon sauce whisk together in cooking pot:
1 cup cold water
1 tablespoon corn starch

Cook on low heat and add:
1 tablespoon lemon juice
1/4 cup honey
1 tablespoon pineapple juice concentrate
1 tablespoon margarine

Stir sauce with wooden spoon for 5 minutes until it thickens and spoon over slices of gingerbread.

Ginger Root

Tummy Mummy

Time: 45 minutes **Serves:** 12

Ready
baking sheet
pastry brush
table knife

Get Set
1 package Pepperidge Farm puff pastry thawed for 20 minutes
small amount of flour
1 egg

For nut stuffing combine following ingredients in a mixing bowl:
1 cup pecan pieces
1/2 cup almond pieces
1/2 cup walnut pieces
1/2 teaspoon of almond extract
1 tablespoon carob powder
3 tablespoons of honey
pinch of cayenne pepper

Go!

1. Open one sheet of Pepperidge Farms puff pastry and lay it out on a floured surface.

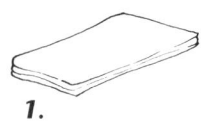

2. Put nut filling in the middle of pastry sheet.

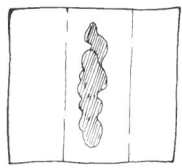

3. Use table knife to cut dough at 45 degree angle.

4. Now braid pastry together.

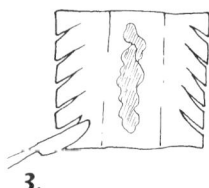

5. Brush on beaten egg with pastry brush.

6. Place on lightly oiled baking sheet.

7. Bake at 350 for about 20 minutes.

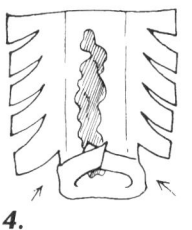

PLAYING WITH FOOD

80

Carrot Sonata

Ready
festive gathering of at least 25 people
recording of Beethoven's 5th Symphony
vegetable peeler
table knife

Get Set
25 peeled carrots

Go!
1. Assemble your guest and give each of them a peeled carrot.

2. Explain to everyone that the fourth note of the symphony is their cue to take a bite of their carrot.

3. Have your group practice biting their carrots at the same time as you sing the first four notes.

4. Everyone should work to make their carrot crunch louder and to crunch in unison.

5. Play your carrot as an instrument!

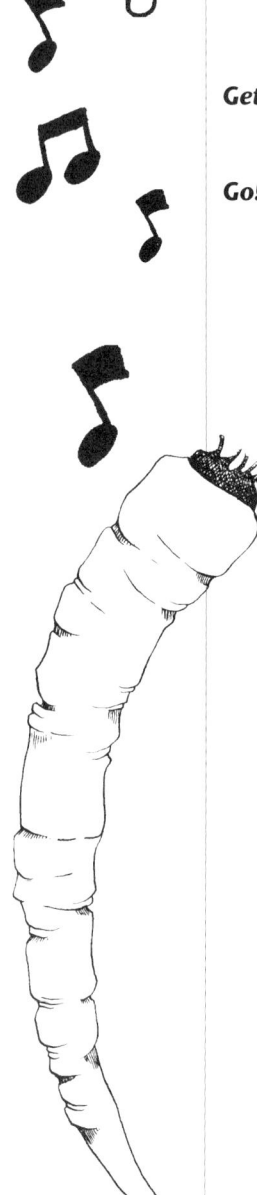

Counterfeit Pizza

Did you know there's a pizza Olympics held every year where "dough throw pros" compete to win prizes for their skill at spinning pizza into the air? These guys play with their food and get paid for it! Here's a good way to throw pizza that won't make a mess.

Time: 15 minutes

Ready
old white bath towel. (Get your parents' permission to use it!)
scissors
round trash can lid
felt marker

Get Set
1. Unfold towel and place trash can lid on top.
2. Draw a circle around the trash can lid with the marker.
3. Remove lid and cut circle from outline of ink on the towel.
4. Clean up scraps of fabric.

Go!
5. Wet circular cloth so it's damp but not dripping.

6. Put both hands underneath cloth.

7. Keep towel horizontal and throw in a clockwise direction up in the air just like a pizza chef.

8. Continue to spin towel with your fingertips in a clockwise direction above your head. You can throw your towel with one hand if you place your fingertips in the middle of pizza and spin it clockwise as it floats back to your hand.

9. You may find another way to toss it, so experiment!

Organize A Kids' Cook-Off

At the Garlic Festival in Gilroy, California, there is a great food stage complete with eight stoves, refrigeration, overhead mirrors, and celebrity chefs. Many people believe this food festival to be the best in the U.S. I had the honor of hosting the first kids cook-off in 1991, where eight kids designed their own pizzas in front of a large audience of hungry people.

If you get good at cooking a certain food, you could compete at a cook-off. If there is a cook-off or bake off in your area, but no kids' competition, ask the executive director to consider having one.

Gravitational Egg

Time: 15 minutes

Ready
1 tall glass with a wide mouth
a small plastic cylinder wide enough to hold an egg in place
clear flat piece of plastic at least 6 x 6 inches

Get Set
1 hard boiled egg

Go!

1. Fill a clear plastic glass 3/4 full of water and place it on the edge of a table.

2. Place a clear piece of plastic on top of the glass.

3. Find a small empty plastic bottle or cylinder that will hold an egg in place.

4. Center the egg so that it is directly above the glass.

5. As you hold the glass knock plastic covering out of the way with one clean strike of your fist.

6. The egg will fall directly into the glass.

1.

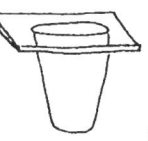
2.

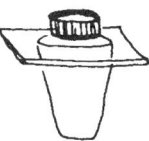
3.

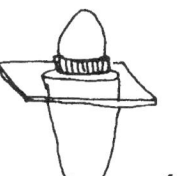
4.

6.

Eggs On Your Breath

Ready
  1 table with smooth surface
  2 players

Get Set
  1 raw egg

Go!
  1. Stab both ends of a raw egg with a toothpick, stabbing yolk inside.

  2. Holding egg over bowl, blow into hole in wide end of egg so liquid oozes out.

  3. Let dry for 10 minutes.

  4. Place at the center of a table so that it is completely still.

  5. Two players try to be the first to blow the egg past their opponents side of the table.

1.

2.

Orange Neck Mutha

Ready
   ten players

Get Set
   two oranges

Go!

1. Form two lines of five players each.

2. Give an orange to both people at the front of the line.

3. Have them place it in between their chin and chest.

4. Without using any hands, players pass the orange to each other using only their necks until it reaches the end of the line.

5. If the orange is dropped players must start again.

6. You can also try this game using elbows, knees, and feet.

Camouflage

Ready
> empty food containers from your pantry with matching lids

Get Set
> something small that you want to hide.

Go!
1. Take used cans or boxes and clean them out and let dry.
2. Deposit your secret valuables inside containers.
3. Place in the back of your pantry and your valuables will be camouflaged.

CHERISH
THE EARTH

Pesticides

Pesticides are poisons used to kill insects and weeds, but they can be dangerous for people too. Many farm workers and their families get sick because they work in fields where these chemicals are used. I try not to eat fruits and vegetables that have been sprayed with pesticides. They not only harm our bodies, but cause pollution as well.

What Can You Do?
1. Buy organic food--food grown naturally without harmful chemicals. Ask your local grocery store to stock organic foods.

2. Buy food from your local farmer's market. Quite often fewer pesticides are used on local produce than fruit and vegetables that are imported from other countries. Farmer's markets have inexpensive prices, friendly people and some of the freshest food in town.

3. Wash your produce thoroughly.

4. Grow your own produce.

5. Write letters to legislators in Congress who can change the laws to protect us. Let them know you're a kid who cares!

6. Buy food that's in season.

7. Buy the freshest, most nutritious food possible.

Recycle And Save A Tree

"Use it up, wear it out, make it do, or do without."
                    Old New England Saying

Good cooks never waste anything: they always recycle!
   Recycling is the process by which we reuse materials that we would otherwise throw out. The most common materials we recycle are glass, paper, aluminum, and plastic but many other materials are also recycled.
   Recycling saves precious space at our landfills, which are quickly running out of room. Recycling also saves natural resources that are in short supply, such as oil, coal and gas.

Don't Forget The Three R's:
Reduce, Reuse, and Recycle!

Ready
   2-3 large washable storage containers

Get Set
   Collect used cans, bottles, glass, paper, and plastic

Go!
   Separate foil, glass, and paper and store them in containers for collection. Many cities provide curbside service on a regular basis. You can also find out where the nearest collection center is located.

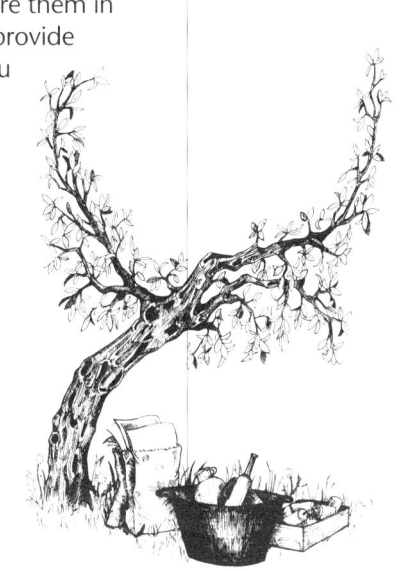

Compost Garden

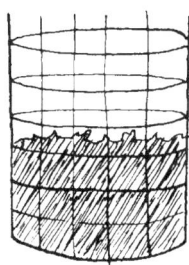

"The Earth does not belong to us, we belong to the Earth."
                              Chief Seattle

Good things compost can do:
   1. It saves landfill space. City dumps are filling up so quickly that some have already run out of space.

   2. It saves money because there is less trash to dump and it can be used as a natural fertilizer in your garden to help things grow.

Ready
   close mesh wire, 1/2 to 1/4 inch between strands, 3 feet wide and 9 feet long, fenced in a circle, or
   use wooden snow fence material.
   shovel or garden fork
   1 pair of pliers

Get Set
   plastic diaper pail or other large container with tight fitting lid.
   leftover kitchen waste, except for meat scraps
   clippings from yard and trees leaves

Go!

1. Locate a place for your compost pile and loosen soil underneath for good drainage.

2. Form fence in a circle and secure edges together with twist ties.

3. Bend any sharp edges of fence downward with pliers so no pointed ends are exposed.

4. Start adding organic materials as they become available.

5. Use things like: grass clippings and leaves, vegetable scraps, coffee grounds, egg shells, banana peels, and rotten food from the refrigerator.

6. Avoid using meat, bones, and fat.

7. Turn the soil in the compost pile once every 2 weeks.

8. Keep pile slightly moist if it begins to dry out.

9. Use the dirt from your compost pile whenever you want to plant anything in your garden.

Rainmaker

Plants can really tell the difference between tap water from your hose and rain that falls from the sky. Some people have built huge storage tanks that catch rainwater and use it in their homes everyday. They never pay a water bill because the rain is free if you figure out how to use it.

Ready
2-3 empty waterproof containers around the house

Get Set
Pray for rain

Go!
1. Once it starts to rain place containers so they will catch the run-off from your roof.

2. After containers are full, cover and save to water your plants.

3. When you water your plants, thank them for being alive!

To order more books send check or money order to:
Piccadilli Press
P.O. Box 50515
Austin, TX 78763
512-453-2051

Quantity	Price	Total
	9.95 each	
Texas residents add 7.75% sales tax (.0775)		
Shipping and handling		1.75
Total enclosed		

Send books to:
Name _____
Address _____
City _____ State _____ Zip _____

GLOSSARY

Additives: Chemicals that are added to preserve freshness, add flavor, color or bind foods together.

Anemia: A condition in which the body is low in red blood cells, resulting in fatigue and pale skin.

Bacteria: Microscopic organisms that feed off air, water, soil, plants, and people.

Bake: To cook using dry heat in an oven.

Baking Soda: A white, crystalline alkali also called bicarbonate of soda and used in baking powder.

Beat: To mix ingredients together thoroughly using circular motion.

Blanch: To plunge into boiling water for only a moment.

Boil: To cook food using heated, bubbling water at 212 degrees Fahrenheit or 100 degrees centigrade.

Boycott: To show disapproval of a product or business by not buying it.

Broil: To cook food directly underneath a flame.

Carbohydrates: Compounds of carbon, hydrogen, and water that come from vegetables. They can be starches, sugars, or fibers.

Cartwheels: Rotelle pasta that are shaped like wheels.

Casein: The principal protein of cow's milk, which is tasteless and odorless.

Cholesterol: A waxy substance that naturally occurs in the bloodstream and in many of the foods that we eat. Small amounts are essential, but excessive amounts can cause heart disease.

Coat: To cover food with sauce or glaze.

Compost: A soil mixture made up of mostly decayed organic matter.

Cream of tartar: An acid that is processed into a white, fine grained substance and used in baking powder.

Dice: To chop in fine pieces.

Dissolve: The chemical process of matter changing from one form to another, such as a dry ingredient being mixed into a liquid solution.

Evaporation: The process of liquid disappearing into vapor.

Fats: Three concentrated sources of energy that can be saturated, found in animal products, dairy products, and eggs. Monosaturated is found in olive, peanut, and canola oils, and other seeds and nuts. Polyunsaturated is found in corn, safflower, sesame, soybean, and wheat germ oil.

Fermentation: A chemical change in food caused by organisms.

Flute: To make a decorative pattern on something like cakes and pies.

Fold: To gently mix delicate ingredients together.

Fungicides: Chemicals used to kill plants and insects.

Garnish: To decorate with food.

Glaze: A substance of sugar or fruit used to cover food for flavor and appearance.

food.

Preservatives: Chemical additives that are used to prevent the decay of food.

Protein: Complex amino acids essential for good nutrition.

Recycle: To use what would otherwise be thrown away.

Reduce: To boil down a liquid to concentrate its flavor and thicken it.

Saturated fat: Waxy substances found in animal and some dairy products that produce cholesterol.

Serrated: A jagged edge found on some knives that allows for easier cutting.

Sift: To push powdered substances through a fine metal screen.

Simmer: To cook at very low heat.

Stand: To let food sit so it will continue to cook after heat has been turned off.

Strain: To pour liquid through a fine metal screen.

Solar Energy: Energy that is furnished by the sun.

Vitamins: Organic chemical compounds that make it possible for our bodies to use the food they take in.

Zest: The outermost rind of a citrus fruit such as a lemon or orange that is removed with a grater.

Grate: To reduce to small particles by rubbing food through a metal device with tiny holes in it.

Grind: To crush to a small powder.

Grill: To cook over direct heat.

Herbicides: A substance that kills plants.

Husk: The outer green leaves that cover an ear of corn.

Immunity: A person's ability to fight disease.

Insecticides: Chemicals used to kill insects.

Landfill: A centralized location to bury trash.

Marinade: The process of using liquids and seasonings to tenderize and add flavor to food.

Microwave: Cooking with electromagnetic waves to heat food.

Mince: To cut into very small pieces.

Nutrition: The science of how people nourish themselves with food.

Organic Food: Food that has been grown without harmful chemicals.

Peel: To remove the outer layer or skin from food.

Pesticides: Chemicals used to destroy pests.

Pinch: A small amount of seasoning put between your thumb and forefinger.

Pollution: To make unclean with human made waste.

Preheat: To ready an oven by turning it on to the desired cooking temperature for ten minutes before cooking